Astral Projection

The Complete Guide for Beginners on Astral Projection, and How to Travel the Astral Plane

Table of Contents

Thank you! _____ 2

Introduction _____ 5

Chapter 1 – Historical References of Astral Projection _____ 7

Chapter 2 - What Exactly Is Astral Projection? _____ 13

Chapter 3 - How Does It Happen? _____ 17

Chapter 4 – How Can You Travel the Astral Plane? _____ 21

Chapter 5 - Understanding the Benefits of Astral Projection 35

Chapter 6 - Can Astral Projection Be Dangerous? _____ 40

Conclusion _____ 42

Check Out My Other Books _____ 44

FREE BONUS! _____ 47

Greetings from the Lean Stone Publishing Company _____ 48

Thank you!

I would like to thank you for buying this book!

If you like the book and get some value out of it, after reading it, I would appreciate if you could leave a positive review on the Amazon Kindle store.

Thank you and enjoy the book!

***

Receive e-mail updates on new book releases and free book promotions from Tabitha Zalot by signing up to the e-mail list by visiting this address: **http://bit.ly/bonus_zalot_cs**

***

Follow us, Lean Stone Publishing, the publishing company that published this book. You will receive e-mail information on upcoming book launches, free book promotions and much more. Sign up to this e-mail list: **http://bit.ly/list_lsp_cs**

***

Like us at **www.facebook.com/leanstonepublishing**

Follow us on Twitter **@leanstonebooks**

©**Copyright 2015 by Tabitha Zalot- All rights reserved.**

This document is geared towards providing exact and reliable information in regards to the topic and issue covered. The publication is sold with the idea that the publisher is not required to render accounting, officially permitted, or otherwise, qualified services. If advice is necessary, legal or professional, a practiced individual in the profession should be ordered.

- From a Declaration of Principles which was accepted and approved equally by a Committee of the American Bar Association and a Committee of Publishers and Associations.

In no way is it legal to reproduce, duplicate, or transmit any part of this document in either electronic means or in printed format. Recording of this publication is strictly prohibited and any storage of this document is not allowed unless with written permission from the publisher. All rights reserved.

The information provided herein is stated to be truthful and consistent, in that any liability, in terms of inattention or otherwise, by any usage or abuse of any policies, processes, or directions contained within is the solitary and utter responsibility of the recipient reader. Under no circumstances will any legal responsibility or blame be held against the publisher for any reparation, damages, or monetary loss due to the information herein, either directly or indirectly.

Respective authors own all copyrights not held by the publisher.

The information herein is offered for informational purposes solely, and is universal as so. The presentation of the information is without contract or any type of guarantee assurance.

The trademarks that are used are without any consent, and the publication of the trademark is without permission or backing by the trademark owner. All trademarks and brands within this book are for clarifying purposes only and are the owned by the owners themselves, not affiliated with this document.

Introduction

I want to thank you and congratulate you for downloading the book, *"Astral Projection – The Complete Guide for Beginners on Astral Projection, and How to Travel the Astral Plane"*.

This book contains proven steps and strategies on how to experiment and have an unbelievable out of body experience through astral projection.

You've surely heard or read at least once about people confessing how, through a near death experience or under the influence of hallucination-inducing drugs, they have traveled outside their body. Or about how their dreams or meditation trances are so intensely vivid that they are capable of feeling and living things that can't be physiologically explained. Regardless of what you have heard before, you've surely wondered if such experiences are actually possible, and if they occur randomly or could be willingly induced. Well, in this book, you will find the precise responses to these questions, and much more.

Since the dawn of time, humans have wondered whether the source of self awareness resides in their bodily form, or is associated with a defined entity only sheltered in it. The existence of spirit has long been debated, but hypotheses and practices that sustain and confirm it abound in veridical details. From real life stories, to religion, culture, and literary works of fiction, a distinction between the physical body and the spiritual body has been clearly made. So, while the first exists solely in the material dimension, the latter can travel outside of it, in its own astral world or astral plane.

Astral projection consists of detaching your spiritual form from the bodily one, and going to places that you could not normally or easily access. Earthly places, but spatial too. In a way, it is a flying and floating activity that allows you to explore a world beyond mundane reach. It is a truly magical adventure you too can embark on after going through this comprehensive guide.

So, if you are eager to connect to your deepest nature, and probe the sense of powerfulness of being in touch with your metaphysical self, look no further. The purpose of this book is to help you better grasp the essence of your life psyche. Moreover, the possibility to astrally project your spiritual body indirectly suggests the verity of life after death claims. What could be more amazing than the idea of implicit eternity? However, you must be aware that astral projection is not recommended for people that suffer from psychological disorders or related issues, as it could impair their distinction between real experiences and out of body occurrences. Other than that, it is a safe and harmless path you can choose to follow in order to better the quality of your life.

Thanks again for downloading this book, I hope you enjoy it!

Chapter 1 – Historical References of Astral Projection

The practice of astral projection can be tracked throughout history thousands of years ago. The concept of acquiring knowledge, enriching personal culture, and enhancing the religious bond with deities through an out-of-body experience (OBE) is clearly explained in various manuscripts and artistic works across many nations. Regardless of the meaning associated with it, the actual travel in astral planes is primarily seen as a valuable step in enlightening and self-awareness.

Inquisitiveness is an innate feature of our species' nature, so it is not surprising that people have always sought to discern a higher significance for living, one that transcends the mortal shell. Based on personal encounters, imaginative exercises, or others' accounts, some people managed to accurately describe the process of spiritual walking or soul travel that astral projection in fact embodies.

Succinctly described below are the most relevant documentations about astral travel that hundreds of generations have produced and passed on from ancient times until present time.

1. Religious doctrines and cultures

The most overwhelming presence of astral projecting implementation can be noted when it comes to the various faithful ideologies manifested across the Earth. The importance of spiritual travel pervades many symbolic representations in cultural lifestyles too, and is not less remarkable in creative reproductions. In fact, anthropological studies have estimated that the majority of cultures that populated the Earth at different times believed to a certain degree in the occurrence of this immaterial experience.

Ancient Egypt - Some claim that the oldest references to astral projection can be found in ancient Egyptian manuscripts. Moreover, it is believed that the great pyramids have been built to facilitate it. Egyptians differentiated five components of the human soul. One of them was Ka, the vital substance or the spirit, which could leave the body at will and travel. However, when the person died, Ka was trapped inside the tomb. Another part was Ba, which could travel the mortal world only after death and venture into the Underworld. Ba kept returning to the tomb until it was possible, when the time came, for it to reunite with Ka in the afterlife.

Chinese Culture - The ancient Taoist religion has been among the first to formulate the idea of a divine self. One meditative practice involves drawing in and focusing the energy spread inside the body, and channeling it to be able to travel and be in different places at the same time.

Indian Religion - In centuries old scriptures of Hinduism, and in Purana texts, it says that magical powers, named Siddhis, can be achieved through meditative and Yoga exercises. One of them, mentioned in the Bhāgavata Purāna is the capacity to undergo astral travel, known as manaḥ-javah, one of the ten secondary Siddhis. There are descriptions of miracles performed through astral projection in the Hindu religion.

On the other hand, Buddhism promotes a principle of reincarnation, where not a clearly defined soul, but a consciousness flow, travels from one life to another in time. However, astral projections in a dream-like state are recalled in this religious doctrine too, as the faithful individuals assumingly can establish a bond with Buddha in an astral plane. There are stories that relate how monks can travel to various levels of heavens, using this form of teleportation, through intense focus and self-discipline.

Roman Empire - The belief that the human spirit is created of a special, unearthly matter, just like the one the stars are made of, was pretty common among many sects in the Roman times, and it was adopted into early Christianity too. Experiences of astral travel displayed in divine visions, and appearances in people's dreams are often mentioned in documents dating back to those times.

In addition, some people believe that certain passages in the Bible make clear suggestions to spiritual travel. It is thought that a high level of devotion, expressed through prayers and strict rites, can help to establish a connection with the astral plane, which is perceived as the place where angels, demons, and other entities exist.

Native Americans - Many tribes of Native Americans also sustained a doctrine of reincarnation and astral projection, noticed by the first travelers in the New World. The so called shamans were the ones who held the secrets of this practice, and they apparently used it to localize herbs used for healing, and find the best places to settle in across the landscape, and to foresee events.

2. *Philosophy and Occultism*

From Plato to Socrates, Pliny, and Plutarch, dreams and experiences that correspond to astral travel have been extensively recorded. The early thinkers and founders of the Western philosophy have expressed their preoccupation with afterlife in their works and mystical views related to the soul and its place in the corporeal reality.

The astral plane is perceived as a middle world of light, between Heaven and Earth, and populated by angelic or demonic entities in philosophical systems popular during the Renaissance, such as Theosophy and Hermeticism. The astral bodies are considered to be components of this plane, and the astral or spiritual body, made of light too, has the role of bonding the physical body to its rational double.

Considered an occult experience by many, in traditions associated with occultism, astral travel is accessed through controlled visualizations and breathing exercises. Often hypnotic-like states and mental representations of a secondary body are used, and the sense of awareness is then voluntarily transferred there.

3. Literature and Art

Prose and Poetry - Many fiction, nonfiction books, and poems have been written about the fascinating subject of astral traveling, but probably the most popular are Dante Alighieri's poetry book, *Divina Commedia*, and Honore de Balzac's fictive work, *Louis Lambert*.

In the last few decades, lots of biographical books relating out-of-body experiences, which initially occurred through near death experiences after surgical interventions or involuntarily, have become available to the public.

Painting - Contemporary exhibitions of astral travel represented on canvas are not ordinary, but not very unusual either. Also, nowadays, a multitude of designs illustrating the individual's journey through this spiritual experience are available online, as paintings or images imprinted on various accessories.

Music - Trance inducing music played with a flute has also been used by Native Americans to facilitate the process of astral projection, and in current times, meditation music is quite common and also sought for the very same purpose. There is also an Israeli band, named Astral Projection that produces a so called psychedelic trance type of electronic music.

4. Modern Science

There are controversial and contradictory statements when it comes to scientifically proving a solid base for astral projection, as many studies and experiments have had various outcomes. While some argue that an out-of-body experience's authenticity can't be determined with practical instruments, and label it as a dream state, others state the opposite and use as evidence the knowledge gathered through psychic means, and the consistent incidence of such cases. Statistically, millions of people have claimed to have lived conscious out-of-body experiences. It has been estimated that one person in ten experiments with it at least once throughout their life.

Out of numerous studies, there are two worthy of mentioning. Their outcomes reinforce indirectly, but indubitably the genuine existence of astral projection occurrences, or at the very least, the actual soul's very state.

In the first research study, a neurologist, Dr. Henrik Ehrsson, used equipment to induce out-of-body experiences and the participants confirmed it. In this particular experiment, screens were placed over the participants' eyes. These screens transmitted images recorded live by cameras placed behind the participants. When the researcher uses two rods to touch a part of their real body and, simultaneously, the same part of their illusory body behind them, they confirmed sitting behind their actual body and noticing their real body from there.

In the second study, dying people where weighted and, after their vital signs stopped, it was observed that their actual weight decreased. This experiment was conducted by Dr Duncan MacDougall in Massachusetts, and his results were published in prestigious medical journals and the New York Times. Apparently, the mass lost in four of the six studied cases was about 21 grams, and ever since, the hypothesis has been widely circulated that this weight corresponds to the weight of the soul. When the physician repeated the experiment with fifteen dogs, no change in the body mass values had been noticed, and he concluded that only humans possess souls.

Many informative surveys have also been created online by researchers of this phenomenon, and the results were extracted from thousands of responses. Most of the internet users that took part in the surveys have declared that they have felt, at least once, one of the common sensations associated with out-of-body experiences. Jolts, sudden low or high frequency sounds, or bodily vibrations are only a few of them.

Chapter 2 - What Exactly Is Astral Projection?

Defining a phenomenon, whose factual existence is based on testimonials, and relevant, but scarce, empirical evidence is open to interpretations. Basically, astral projection is an out-of-body experience that engages the sensorial system and whose effects are mostly of a psychological nature. The platform on which it relies is not necessarily related to beliefs or desires, but is dependent on sensitive self-awareness. However, its long-term usage and the mostly positive consequences resulting from such incidents support its high relatedness among humans.

Astral projection, regardless of the causes and intentions associated with it, voluntarily or involuntarily, is an experience that fascinates and stimulates our minds and imaginations, as it is an outstanding route one can follow to personal enlightenment. It represents feasible proof that the significance of our lives could rise above terrestrial limitations. It's also a manner to confront and defeat the fears of uncertain circumstances, and the unknown, that so many times extends beyond our control.

In the following paragraphs, you will discover the most important interpretations, whose validity cannot be contested in relation to astral projection.

Supernatural Affair

Beyond religious, cultural, and spiritual interpretations, astral projection is a supernatural manifestation in which one's astral body separates from the physical one, and travels through higher or lower dimensions, or around the physical world.

It is assumed that the fifth dimension is the one usually chosen, the extra dimension that is the subject of many astrophysics and mathematics preoccupations. We live in a 4-dimension world, three spatial and one time dimension. Hypothetically, the concept of a fifth dimension could mean an alternative world in which one could make different life choices and travel into.

The astral plane of existence can be inhabited by various entities or can be unpopulated. The journey can be made in different times and spaces, and during its unfolding, the astral body's connection with the physical body is not ceased and cannot be broken. A silver cord or astral cord maintains, at all times, the bond between the two.

Because other astral bodies can coexist in the same astral plane, the encounters with them are considered very probable. Furthermore, if the astral plane is composed of spheres associated with hells, heavens, and other ethereal spaces occupied by beings such as angels, demons, or specters, it is possible to interact and communicate with them too. Hence, astral projection can prove to be not only an individual, but also a social affair.

Art of Transcendent Liberation

Astral projection is the proper art of detaching one's consciousness from their material self and transferring it to the spiritual one. Then, through discipline and concentration, the astral body is capable of leaving its shelter, the mortal form, and traveling away from it. Its liberation is meant to enrich and release, through transcendent elevation and cognition, its possessor. It's the pursuance of that feeling, materialized in random thoughts, such as "I just wish I could fly away from everything and release myself of my worries! Just be totally free!", which we all can relate to at some point in time.

Even though it is teachable and malleable, astral projection can occur during sleep time too. That is because the astral body can follow the subconscious wishes of the person to whom it belongs. So, at times, if the intensity of one's desire is powerful enough, through the realm of dreaming, one can perceive an out-of-body experience too. In this case, it is meant as an act of fulfillment of real aims that otherwise might not be accessible or unperceived.

"Last Act" Anticipation

Intimately associated with reincarnation and afterlife, astral projection can be employed as a valuable instrument in studying the dying process. No, it is not meant to enhance the gloominess one might feel when thinking about the last act our corporeal bodies undergo in the earthly world. It is an anticipative model, whose purpose is to help you comprehend this natural, inevitable process, and even to embrace it when your time finally comes. In fact, it can easily be viewed as a sort of simulation of the finale. The only major difference is that when the physiological demise occurs, the astral body's connection with the physical body is severed.

Near death experiences stand as solid attestations for the reliability astral projection possesses when it comes to researching the physical death. Most of the people who have come across such crucial events have reported going through out-of-body episodes, and clearly seeing the image of the physical figure left behind. The essential fact to retain from these accounts is that, after living through these incidents, and getting back into their bodies, these people have lost all their fears related to death. The euphoric state they reached during their near death experiences, through floating and flying in spiritual form away from their bodily form, is the same that people Describe who willingly practice astral projection.

Lastly, an important fact to acknowledge is that, even though it can be felt in various ways by different people, astral projection is essentially the same phenomenon. Whether it's discerned as religious illumination, personal insight, or a path to salvation from mortal anxieties and pressures, astral projection is an extraordinary manner to progress on all levels of your existence, and evolve your individuality.

Chapter 3 - How Does It Happen?

So, now that you know what astral projection means, how it can be used, and in what particular situations it can be triggered, it is time for you to find out how it works. How does it happen? How can one differentiate it from a vision generated by a wish for it to happen, or from a dream in which it appeared to have happened? Well, accidental or intentional, this phenomenon is naturally designed in steps, that, with small variations from a person to another, indicate its passage.

1. Pre-Astral Projection Indicators

Before the astral journey begins, a series of symptoms of physical and psychological nature, announce that the experience is about to happen. These signs constitute a preparation process for your body and mind, so as to make possible the spiritual projection. Your focus shifts from surroundings to inner perceptions and your self-awareness is awakened.

Sensorial Signs - When one prepares for, or spontaneously is close to experiment an astral travel, they will often *hear sudden sounds* of various intensities, such as humming, buzzing, or howling. It is also possible to perceive actual voices or other sounds such as of objects falling. However, the buzzing noise is the most commonly signaled, and, in some cases, can rise to barely tolerable levels.

Another sensation that can and does happen in anticipation of the astral projection is *optical hallucinations.* Before your physical body enters the specific trance state for the astral body to undergo its journey, you can see things. These can range from mixtures of colors and patterns of shapes to fantastic scenes and visions. Some people can see a tunnel and a light at its end, a common depiction in near-death experiences.

Catalepsy, sleep paralysis, or bodily rigidity, is also a common pre-indicator of astral travel. The feeling that your body can't move is many times associated with the inability to speak. It can be scary, but this is often assimilated with a dream-like state and in fact, if no fear shadows it, it relaxes the body.

Modifications such as *irregular or fast heartbeats* can also be experienced. It might be due to a rush of emotion, such as uneasiness or elation, or an initiatory requirement. A clear explanation doesn't exist, but it doesn't seem to influence the subsequent voyage negatively.

Shortness of breath can be felt too, but, just as the increased heart rate, it's a symptom that usually subsides as soon as you proceed with the astral projection.

Psychosomatic Signs - Besides physical changes that indicate the development of an out-of-body experience, significant psychological happenings add to the body's preparation for its spiritual travel component.

The most familiar sign in this category is related to movements. Not physical movements, but movements that are internally perceived. Specifically defined as *vibrations,* these progressive little waves, felt throughout your body, without actually any physical response, are believed to represent the most defining symptom of astral projection.

Another psychosomatic sign that supports the suggestion of further astral travel is *dizziness*. A sensation of falling, flying, or being suspended typically dominate in this case. It directly implies that your astral body is ready to be released from its bodily confinement.

A *weight shift* feeling can accompany the emotional manifestations that precede your astral projection. You can suddenly become aware of the fact that your body feels heavy or very light, as if your bodily mass has dropped or has suddenly risen.

Bodily temperature fluctuation can as well be discerned. A coldness sensation or, on the contrary, a heat flush can come over you.

2. The Actual Process

When the astral body detaches from the physical body, one is clearly aware of it. Unlike the case when you dream or self-induce a state of vision, you often notice your bodily self laying on the bed after you rise above it, and sometimes the cord that connects you to it is visible too. Also, the surrounding details keep their integrity. Unlike in a dream or vision, where alterations to the material world happen, during the actual astral journey, everything related to the physical world you are traveling in and across, is unchanged. You won't find yourself in a strange place all of a sudden, but will travel there from your detachment moment. This is a fundamental element that distinguishes astral projection from sought after visualizations and dreams.

The astral body is not affected by gravity and its ethereal manifestation is not governed by other physical laws. So, it can fly, float, or fall. Also, even though it can travel through the material world, your spiritual form isn't capable of touching objects or beings or feeling them. So, it will go through them. Yes, that means passing through walls and people. However, when it comes to objects and creatures that inhabit the astral plane, the astral body can feel, touch, and acknowledge them, just as the earthly body does in the physical world. So, your thinking processes and senses do not get lost, but they get applied to another level.

Because there are no actual rules or limits in the astral dimensions, it is mostly what you make of it. Your mind models it, and your feelings determine most of the experiences that occur in the astral plane. Notions as up, down, left, and right are perceived only because your mindset is contouring them, based on your physical existence. Furthermore, your vision is in fact, an all-encompassing 360 degrees view. Also, there are distinct energetic levels that you can reach on the astral plane dependent on your thoughts and intentions. The entities you come into contact with usually inhabit different levels based on their similarities too.

3. Post-Astral Projection Indicators

Just as there are certain triggering symptoms that lead to astral projection, there also are specific signs that occur at the end of this spiritual journey. These signs, as they mark the end of an astral journey, have a psychological impact, and seldom manifest physiologically.

Vivid *recollections* from the travel usually indicate its occurrence. It can be argued that these can be the results of an imaginative process, but when astral projecting during a wakeful state is engaged, even though not tangible, these can illustrate loyal representations from the material world, and also from the astral plane.

A pervading sense of total *calmness* has been noticed often in people that went through out-of-body experiences. Whether this is a side effect, prompted by the consequent grasp of one's boundless spiritual existence, or a direct impact caused by the temporary release of the spiritual self, its presence has been widely affirmed.

Some people apparently develop *healing and foretelling* abilities, through learning to channel their inner energies in positive astral projections. It is generally assumed that unleashing one's awareness in higher dimensions can allow one to overrule the limitations enforced on their overall being by the physical existence.

Chapter 4 – How Can You Travel the Astral Plane?

As it has been previously mentioned, some people get to travel spiritually without any intention, while finding themselves in critical situations, induced by circumstances such as near-death experiences and dreams. Meanwhile, other people do it intentionally, whether by means of intense practice (meditation, self-discipline), or using additional help (hypnosis, hallucinogenic drugs, research studies). This guide is elaborated to provide you the exact information on how to prepare and travel the astral plane through self-thought practice.

Possible enhancers, which are helpful and harmless instruments that can help you facilitate the astral projection, will be indicated here too. However, you must keep in mind that the most important tool in order to succeed is your will. As long as you truly desire to experiment with this phenomenon, and have decided to channel your energy towards achieving this goal, no substantial impediment can stop you from doing so. The only barriers are the ones your own mind creates, but you will also be advised here about how you can release yourself from anxieties and doubts and strengthen your motivation.

Step by step, you will now learn how to safely adventure on an astral journey in realms that you have only imagined or dreamed about. Firstly, you need to get yourself ready physically and mentally, then try the most popular techniques described below, and, based on the outcome, select the one that suits you best. Because our personalities differ, and we possess distinct levels of awareness and imaginative capability, the only way to figure out the most effective method for you is to test the few renowned ones presented here. Lastly, you need to stick with the one you feel most comfortable with, and develop your astral travel skills from there.

Physical Preparation

It is very important for the setting in which your out-of-body experience happens to be safe, convenient, and relaxed, so that no worldly disturbances will occur and affect the success of your spiritual projection.

Surroundings - Usually, the most recommended location would be your bedroom, the *place* where you should feel most protected and at peace with yourself. But if you don't live alone, and you share your most intimate space with someone else, it is not a good idea, as it can easily get you distracted. So, in this case, the thing to do is choose another room. Whether it is in your own home or somewhere else, it is crucial for this place to be safe.

It is ideal that your location is not in the middle of a busy area, or nearby a rail station or airport, as noises can make it hard for you to ignore the background and focus on your internal processes. However, if these can't be avoided, use soft earplugs or earphones. Yes, it will further be explained how music can be incorporated in your mental preparation for the astral travel.

Close the windows, lock the door, and check that devices such as mobile or home phone, TV, and others are turned off. Also, make sure no one will actually come around during this time, invited or not. You wouldn't want to be interrupted at the exact moment when you are about to take off into the astral plane, would you?

The best *time* of the day to practice astral projecting is very early in the morning. Some people do it during the night too, but it is more likely that your mind is lucid and capable of focusing after a good night's rest. This time frame is also desirable, because human activity is almost nonexistent before dawn, so the peacefulness around you can only assist your spiritual endeavor.

Another important element of your surroundings is the *temperature*. It depends on the season, but you should regulate the heating or the air conditioning so as to create a slightly warm atmosphere. This is because your bodily temperature often drops while your astral body travels away from your material body.

Body - When it comes to *clothing*, opt for loose and soft attire. Your casual pajamas will do. Otherwise, you can also wear nothing at all, but in that situation, you should cover your body with a light blanket or sheet, as it could get cold while its astral double travels away.

A very common *position* of one's physical body, when getting ready for a voluntary out-of-body experience, is lying on the bed on your back, while keeping the limbs stretched, forming a continual line. Your eyes should be closed so they will not be attracted to details in your vicinity.

The next thing to do is *relax your muscles*. Loosen whatever tension might be in them, and become aware of all your parts, from head to toe. Gradually advance from forehead to your neck, chest, back, and tummy, while going through each limb. Move slowly, and then fully relax.

The *breathing* should be deep and slow. Inhale and exhale without rush, and release the stiffness that might be accumulated in your chest and shoulders. Embrace a sluggish, yet steady pattern.

Mental Preparation

When your body is fully relaxed and has reached a similar state as the one preceding sleep, you must prepare your mind accordingly to stay focused and alert. That is because when you are astral projecting, your body enters a sleep mode, the difference being that your mind doesn't accompany it, but remains awake. Simply, what you must obtain in order to astral travel is a modified condition of awareness. The mental consciousness is active and accompanying your astral body, while your physical body remains in an inactive state, as when sleeping.

Relaxation - Our mind wanders all the time, and the most pregnant thoughts are the ones related to worries, problems to solve, things to do, targets to achieve, and so on. It is a scientifically proven fact that many of us tend to fret over the most insignificant details and events that are part of our earthly existence. So, how does one relax while keeping their body still? How can this be done in order to further allow particular focus on a transcendent phenomenon? Well, read further and you will find out the responses to these questions.

Music - Different music genres have sounds emitted at various frequencies, and their effect on the brainwaves is consequently varied. Isochronic tones, along with monaural and binaural tones, have been studied and concluded to represent stimuli that determine a frequency change inside the human brain, which leads to hemispheric synchronization. This condition is apparently correlated with health benefits such as high concentration, control over pain, and stress management. It is the reason why people that meditate or practice astral projection listen to relaxation music with these beats.

Essential Oils - It has been remarked that certain essential oils have the capacity to enhance psychic experiences. Whether applied directly on your skin, in certain areas such as forehead, wrists, the back of the neck, and ankles, or kept in a diffuser that spreads their scent, these plant extracts can help you relax completely. Most frequently, frankincense, cinnamon, jasmine, myrrh, and rosemary derived oils are the ones selected.

Herbs - Prepared as teas and consumed before comfortably positioning your body on the bed for the subsequent astral projection, or stuffed in small sacks that release their scent, many herbs with protective, healing, and relaxing effects can be reliable additional helpers.

Probably the most popular herb utilized to ease astral projection is moonwort, widely employed for prophecies and guardianship during the ancient times. Associated with witchcraft and apparently omnipresent in flying ointments, its genus name, "Artemisia", derives from the Greek goddess of the moon, Artemis. Other herbs include honeysuckle, valerian, bay, wintergreen, chamomile, and eyebright.

Crystals - Certain gemstones have also been deployed for travel in the astral plane, as some have calming and stress releasing properties. Fear, anxiety, and irritability of all sorts can be kept at bay or simply cast away with the help of crystals such as prehnite, aventurine, blue calcite, lithium quartz, sugilite, and magnesite.

Concentration - After removing all the potential mental obstacles through relaxation, it is necessary to channel the mind in the particular direction it needs to enter into astral projection. Focus is a key factor preceding the practical access into astral realms through spiritual detachment. As long as your motivation is solid and you thoroughly relaxed your mind and body, there is no actual reason that could prevent you from centralizing your awareness on a single track.

Autosuggestion - The easiest way to gather your streams of consciousness into a uniform flux, and to center your thinking on the out-of-body-experience you are about to live, is by means of autosuggestion. Engage your inner voice and direct your thoughts towards positive self-assurance. Repeat as if they were religious prayers or a magical rite's brief sentences, such as "I am going to do it, I will travel in the astral plane", "I will succeed with my astral projection", or "I am gifted and I will ascertain my out-of-body experience".

It might seem a bit silly or futile at first, but remember what you read before. Your will and state of mind dictate your actual capability. Don't let doubts and impatience take a hold on you. Saying and repeating, while strongly believing, extends your self-awareness and eventually leads to achievement.

Imaginative self-observation - Mostly a meditative exercise, this focus challenge engages your creative power. Remember that astral projection, just as any other significant pursuit, is an art. To discover new worlds, it is important to discern their nuances, shapes, and textures. In this case, your mind is the canvas on which you paint, so you learn to distinguish clearly. The more you use it, the more likely you are to create the essential mental gate through which you can release your spiritual form. But no, there is no need to actually imagine the new world.

Instead, here is what you have to do. With your eyes closed, and your body relaxed as much as possible, you imagine a part of your body that is moving. You meditate over this image until it feels as vivid as a real one. Physically, you don't move, let's say your arm or foot, but mentally, you create a powerful image of it moving. Then, you channel your energy in it. By means of power, will, and imagination, you collect all the vital energy scattered inside your body and concentrate it in your limb. From that site, you can engage one of the techniques succinctly presented in the following paragraphs to liberate your spiritual being.

Top 10 Easiest and Most Effective Astral Travel Techniques

Many techniques of astral projection have been developed across history, but the suitability of each of them for one individual or another cannot be guaranteed. However, there are a few effective methods that most people have recorded success with, and those are described below for you to select from, according to your needs and skills. Of course, in order to establish the right one for you, you must attempt them all, but that shouldn't constitute a problem, as the whole process doesn't usually require more than a few minutes, ten at most. However, you shouldn't devote a single day to try them all. Use them gradually, one at a time.

1. The Visualization Technique

This meditation method is probably the easiest way to astral projection. It is mainly a matter of directed focus, and it engages your mind's power to visualize. Just as when concentrating, you visualize something real. It could be your own body, another person, an object situated in your close proximity, or a location where you intend to astral travel. All other unrelated thoughts must be ignored and pushed aside.

If you visualize your *physical body*, then you must create its corresponding spiritual double. Then slowly, you begin to move it part by part above your real figure, and progressively involve your whole astral body. Your purpose is to visualize the transfer of your physical perceptions to your spiritual form. The next thing to do is float. Yes, you imagine seeing your astral body floating above your physical one. Your sense of physical awareness will gradually attenuate until the vibrations will take over. Regardless, you keep your focus on imagining your spiritual body hovering above, and watching your physical body from there. Eventually, as the vibratory state intensifies, your astral shape is released and you can see your relaxed, real body in a state of relaxed sleep beneath you, and the silver cord attaching you to it.

If you visualize *another person or an object* present in your room, you should be aware of their precise location. Then, you literally set your mind on reaching the other person or the object. In your astral form, you exit from the physical body and project yourself in the material world at first. From there, you can adventure in the astral plane only by thinking of it.

If you visualize *an actual place,* whether you've traveled there before or not, you must have at least a photograph that you can study. Memorize the landscape and, after relaxation, picture yourself exiting your body and flying inside the actual place. Preceded by the overall vibrations, your astral body will liberate itself and reach for the place. And so, your explorations begin.

2. The Mirror Technique

This method can be a great way to improve your visualization skills. It involves a real mirror, one in which you can see your whole body, that must be placed where it allows you to see your full reflection. Observe every detail of your body clearly, from head to toe, while taking in the surroundings too. Notice its shape, its position, and practice little movements. Your centre of attention is your reflection. Examine it as if it's a painting or drawing you must reproduce.

After a while, close your eyes, but keep the image still. Focus on the way your body is reflected in the mirror, its exact outline, the lights or shadows on it. Begin to move your reflection's body as your own body moves: your fingers, your eyes, your arms and legs. Keep your body relaxed until it reaches a state of sleep, while you visualize your reflection.

Then, imagine rising from your bed and walking around the room. Feel the bare floor or the soft, warm carpet beneath your feet. Pay attention to all the sensations associated with your movement. Your breathing, the objects you see, the contraction, and relaxation, of your moving muscles. As you do so, the transfer of awareness from your sleepy body to your astral one, the mirror's reflection, will occur. You will then perceive new details around you and things that you haven't noticed or paid attention to before. The color or fabric of an item, the positioning of a piece of furniture compared to another, etc. Maintain your calmness and enjoy the new sensations.

3. The Rope Technique

Originally developed by Robert Bruce, a famous astral projection practitioner, this technique is mostly based on tactile sensations. So, if you don't have a well-developed visual memory, but your imagination is not a problem when it comes to sensory feelings, this might be the one for you.

The central object in this case is a rope - an imaginary one that you must mentally project as hanging from the ceiling. Using the imaginary hands of your astral form, you reach towards it and then pull yourself up on it. Hand over hand, you advance with your climbing, and a feeling of vertigo will now begin to build up in your body. Do not stop. Keep focusing on the strong rope, whose texture and width you can sense, and on your ascension. As you do so, you will soon feel vibratory waves going through your body. Continue to climb. Further, you will perceive your astral body coming out of your physical body and reaching for the rope. Next, released of it, it will float above, around the ceiling. And your astral journey now begins.

4. The Ladder Technique

Practically, this technique is very similar to the previous one, but in this case you will use a ladder. This is more indicated if you don't feel you could handle such a task in real life, or that you couldn't rely exclusively on your upper body parts to climb up something. So, a ladder that ends near the ceiling is the object you aspire to climb on until you reach its top.

Using your feet and hands too, you follow the same steps described in the rope technique until you manage to finally liberate your astral body.

5. The Swing Technique

Just as the name suggests, this technique involves another object, a swing. For this method, as for the ladder and rope ones, you can actually experience the real sensations by real life attempts. This way, the feelings of the actual motion will be easier to recall and build up with your imagination.

Completely relaxed, and in a state of deep concentration, just as before, you imagine a swing on which you sit. Be aware of the way your hands grasp the swing's ropes, acknowledge the way your feet dangle in the air beneath you. As you begin your movement, focus on the air that gently brushes your face and moves through your hair. Move faster and feel the air's pressure against your chest, the whizzing in your ears, and the slight tension in your shoulders. While swinging higher and higher, you will perceive signs signaling the further projection. Unusual sounds, electric vibration, shortness of breath. As these occur, picture yourself suddenly falling or flying up from the moving swing. It is the moment when your exit happens. Detach your astral body from your physical one, and proceed to traveling where you initially intended to.

6. The Tunnel Technique

This method involves an image whose popularity is widespread in accounts of involuntary out-of-body experiences such as near death experiences. The vision's central element is not the tunnel itself, but the light at the end of it. As you probably anticipate, the light is what you endeavor to reach.

Draw a mental picture of a tunnel, and then visualize yourself entering it. At the beginning, you will be surrounded by complete darkness, but little by little, its presence will feel reassuring. Move through it step by step, aiming for its end, the light, which might seem like a faraway point. As you intensify the light's sparkle and its dimension, also increase your pace. If you started walking, progress to running. Run fast as if you were in a race, and at the end, imagine yourself flying or floating into the light. Usually, the actual separation will be assisted by its precursory symptoms and will materialize when you leave the tunnel.

7. The Fall Technique

The free falling technique is in fact very simple. Unrelated to surroundings or external representations, this one is exclusively focused on your actual body, just like the visualization one.

While lying comfortably and relaxed on your bed, and almost reaching the near the trance state, try to become aware of the solid mattress beneath you. Feel the way your body is pressed against its even surface.

Then, focus your mind on causing a falling sensation. Envisage your body falling through the bed, through the floor, even through the earth. At first, do it slowly: your palms sinking down a little, then your heels. Continue until half of your horizontal body is below the line of the bed sheet. The weight of the body becomes less and less material, as if made of an ethereal matter. Then, sink further, increasing the speed of your falling. Do it until your astral body falls out of your actual body, hitting the ground, or the specific symptoms of projections take over. In the latter case, continue until you stop falling and find yourself defying gravity, flying, or floating above your actual body, still and asleep on the bed.

8. The Jump Technique

Similar to the free falling and visualization techniques, the jump method also involves your body and inducing an image of its moving. It is based on the fact that, while the real body obeys gravity and other laws of physics, the astral one isn't restricted by material limits. In real life, when you jump, you end up landing on the ground. When you astral travel, you fly, rotate, or float into the air, as the material ground is not necessary to support your immaterial mass.

The first step is to simply jump while awake. You will obviously hit the ground. Continue to do so during the day as to convince yourself that you are moving in the real world.

Then, early in the morning or after a nap, when you're relaxed and rested, you can decide to astral project. Let yourself reach the needed sleepy state. What's more, allow yourself to fall asleep this time. While your awareness, of course, is maintained alert. Remember, a real out-of-body experience through astral projection is a conscious choice that involves an awake mind and a mostly asleep body.

As you enter the dreams realm, with your consciousness still in an active state, make yourself jump, just as you did during the day in real life. This time, you won't hit the ground. So, through your lucid dreaming, you get out of your body and astral project. Your proof is your conscious jump. Begin to explore the fantastic realm in which you find yourself.

9. The Roll out Technique

When we sleep, we tend to roll over to one side or the other. Whether to reach a more comfortable position, or while dreaming, we often find ourselves in different postures when waking up. The roll out technique is based specifically on that.

Engaging your will and imagination, you project your astral body rolling to the right or the left. Make sure you do keep your physical body still and relaxed as required. As you focus on the rolling movement that your spiritual double undertakes, you will soon reach a dizziness state, and the typical vibrations will emerge. The separation will finally occur, and your astral form will roll out of your corporeal form.

10. The Muldoon's Thirst Technique

Practitioner and author in the field of astral projection, Sylvan Muldoon, developed this technique, taking in consideration one of most intense physical demands, thirst. This method entails a factual state of your real body: deprivation of water.

For a couple of hours before attempting astral travel, do not consume fluids at all. Then, a bit before beginning the process, place a glass or bottle of water in the vicinity of the place where the actual phenomenon will occur. It is even recommended to eat a bit of salt, or a food with high salt content to amplify your craving for drinking water.

After going into your relaxation state, concentrate your attention on your thirst and picture yourself getting up, walking to the nearby source of alleviation, and lifting it up. Step by step, repeat these processes until you reach the dreamy state. Then, as the specific signs take over your actual body, the astral one will eventually liberate itself and reach for the bottle or glass of water.

In a modified version, where no actual source of water is utilized, your astral body might lead you to another source of water from the real world.

How Long Does It Take?

Astral projecting is a spiritual occurrence that each and every one of us can experience, but the time required for a successful travel differs individually. For some it takes weeks, for others months, while there are people that effectively travel on their first attempt. The crucial thing is that you must not get discouraged or feel desolate over it, you need to persist and strengthen your belief in the process. Often, the unconscious doubts and fears are the ones that obstruct us from connecting with our spiritual double, and validate its presence by its liberation from the material form. However, by means of constant practice and deep commitment, the access will be made in time.

When it does happen, note the amount of time spent outside your physical body. As you become more familiar and skilled in astral travel, your capability to control the phenomenon and the necessary time for it will significantly grow. If at the beginning you find yourself spending seconds in the astral realm, you can go as far as tens of minutes. Take into consideration that the notions of time and space are applicable only in the real world, so a few seconds in the physical world might feel like days or weeks in the astral plane.

Chapter 5 - Understanding the Benefits of Astral Projection

The benefits of astral projection extend beyond our material existence. You might decide to attempt traveling in the astral plane out of a sense of curiosity, religiosity, or eagerness for a supernatural experience. Or you might in fact want to find some answers about yourself, or something that happened or happens to you. Whatever your reason might be, you will receive much more than you hoped for. Because the profound modification that astral projection can cause in your being, influences not only your mental and emotional perceptions of life, death, and meaning, but your physical world as well. Below, you will find the 10 most important and precious rewards you will gain in your spiritual journey.

1. Metaphysical Awakening

Living in a universe governed by laws, and self-imposed, or otherwise imposed boundaries can feel a bit frustrating or stifling at times. Making a connection with your astral self, and awakening your divine perceptions, shatters all the limits that restrict you in the material world. If you are a faithful person, this will directly affect your spirituality, and facilitate a direct bond with your adored one(s). If, on the contrary, your belief vibrates in the energy flow scattered within your being, you will reach the deepest levels of self-awareness and the most intimate knowledge about your being's meaning. This effect depends on your personal ideology, but its ultimate contribution is the same: producing the unswerving liberation of your metaphysical consciousness.

2. Enhanced Imagination

Because it continually provokes your ordinary views and your creative potential, by means of visualization, detailed examination and concentration on natural or fantastic elements, astral travel augments your imagination. The more you practice it, the more you will be inclined to break free from the common paths and patterns of thinking, and the immediate result will be seen in your productivity. Imagination is what we engage to evolve beyond our bodily confinement, but it's also the essential tool for finding real life solutions for various types of problems. So this considerable advantage will greatly reflect in your real life choices too, and it can only lead to positive and prosperous outcomes.

3. Extrasensory Abilities

Properties such as healing, telepathy, and foretelling are usually characteristics in legends, fairytales, and intensely debated accounts. The truth is, all of them are attainable. Through astral projection, as you align and unite your constituent parts, the astral and physical bodies, you remove all the emotional blockages that impeded you before from grasping your surroundings beyond mundane intuition. As you become skilled in traveling in higher energetic levels, and the frequencies on which you emit and receive signals from the bodies around you advance, it is possible to communicate with other beings at mystic levels. Whether they reside in the material or spiritual realm, you can bond with them, and influence their health state and yours, be it corporeal or emotional.

4. Liberation of Death Fears

How many times have you looked up into the sky and wished you were a bird, free of your gravity obeying bodily mass, able to fly up high? And how many times did you tremble within, at the thought of your inevitable ending on this earth? You've surely wondered about death and dreaded its apparently decisive power. When you fly into spiritual worlds you only dreamed about, you not only fulfill a dream of unrestrained-to-ground liberty, but you also release yourself from the fears of the finale. Because you discover that it's really nothing to fear, but rather to embrace. It's a weightless flight, an unbounded journey, during which regrets of lost time and longings for faraway spaces never occur. As time and space and outer laws don't exist anymore, the only barriers are the ones your spirits sets.

5. Life after Death Confirmation

An out-of-body experience doesn't just disclose that there is nothing to fear about the final detachment of your spiritual body from your physical one, but also reveals death is the final stop for your worldly shape. It's basically an astral projection that isn't followed by returning to your material form, as the silver cord that kept you tied to it has broken. Your very essence, the soul, lives on, and, if desired, it can actually return in another suitable earthly figure. Or it can fly up into your personal heaven and live happily there for an eternity.

6. Personal Growth

Most of the people that went through near-death experiences, or other similar involuntary out-of-body incidents, declared how their perspective on living and its quality changed. Traveling in the astral plane not only consolidates your self-assurance and incites unsuspected powers and abilities, but it also elevates you. If our personal development was a pyramid, the ideal state would be reached at the top. How many people expect to actually touch their highest aspirations? And how many actually do? It is easy to respond to these questions if you consider that most of them never progress beyond earth-bound circumstances. But when one dwells and ponders beyond that, the respect for life in its complete unfolding will sharpen. And so will the empathy and the love for self and others, which is what helps guide your steps to the highest level of the pyramid.

7. Time Travel

Remember, time and space are material representations, and valid only for a universe whose mass can be evaluated. Since in the astral plane, time doesn't exist, you can move in whatever dimension you wish. So, going back or forth, moving between past and future, while your physical body is caught in the present is not an unrealistic objective anymore. From ancient times to the Renaissance, and from there all the way to current times and a futuristic after time, you can visit them all. Obviously, this will not happen on your first attempt at astral projection, because your skills must be suitably developed. Still, this is possible.

8. Retrospective Comprehension

By traveling in time and space, even getting to meet yourself while in previous lives, you can obtain explanations for the way you are, who you are, and what your actual purpose is for your actual existence. Or you can simply find out something from the not faraway past, something that perhaps occurred in your childhood, and you want to explore and understand it. Whatever your aim, through astral projection, you can better realize a meaning, or a fact that previously might have seemed senseless, distressing, or too dull.

9. Tonic Relaxation

As you get in tune with yourself, and practically solve the mysterious puzzle of your own biography, you will gradually achieve an unparalleled state of relaxation. No disturbance will affect you as it used to before, and no obstacle will ever afflict you that much to make you feel defenseless and defeated. A peaceful sentiment will accompany you wherever you go, as long as you maintain a smooth communication with your spiritual self, and banish all the passing and damaging concerns.

10. Complete Self-Coordination

Because your energy flow is uninterrupted and your every pore, whether physical or spiritual, is coordinated with the surrounding ones, your inner organization will be impeccable. And it will reflect in your outer one accordingly. Discipline and orderly arrangement are key factors for achieving success and fulfilling aspirations, as perseverance is usually associated with them. Through astral projection, you will acknowledge exactly what you are looking for, the means to obtain it, and you will structure your endeavors to satisfy your inner and outer purposes.

Chapter 6 - Can Astral Projection Be Dangerous?

There are many people out there expressing fears about the potential dangers astral projection might bring about, but most of their fears are related to personal anxieties, and not proven occurrences. However, it is normal to fret over something you are not familiar with, especially when it involves an intense involvement in the process. Moreover, even though it is similar for most people, individually it can manifest differently. The 5 most common fears related to astral travel, and their necessary clarifications, are addressed in the following paragraphs.

1. Can One Be Possessed During Astral Projection?

Entities of all types reside in the astral realm, some of them malicious, others angelic. The first ones' energy is low, the latter's is high. It is believed that vibrating at very low energetic levels can allow demonic beings to attempt to possess one's physical body when they are away astral traveling. However, in order for them to do so, most of the time, you will have to invite them to. If you don't, and you don't seek to astral travel to mainly escape your physical body, but to explore your astral one, there is no reason to fear. A strong connection with your body will not permit any other being to enter it. It is perfectly built for you only.

2. Is It Possible To Die While Astral Traveling?

The silver cord that ties your astral and physical body can not normally be severed, broken, or stretched to the point of breaking. Normally, no foreign astral body can cut it. On the other hand, your physical body is vulnerable while you astral travel, in the sense that it can be harmed in ways that could happen during sleep. That's why it is of uttermost importance to astral project in a very safe place.

3. Will You Always Return Safely To Your Physical Body?

Your physical body is the home of your astral body, so you will never forget the way back to it. In fact, this is only a matter of will. In an instant, if you imagine it, you can return to your body from wherever you might have projected yourself.

4. Can You Get Blocked In The Astral Plane?

No, unless you let yourself be overwhelmed by fears of getting lost or blocked. Your mental state is in charge of the things that happen to you. So, if you remain strong and confident at all times, there is no reason to believe that you will get stuck outside your body.

5. Does Your Physical Body Get Exhausted Because Of It?

At the end of an astral projection, your body will actually feel as refreshed and rested as after a good night's sleep. Only your spirit is engaged in the astral voyage.

***

Receive e-mail updates on new book releases and free book promotions from Tabitha Zalot. By visiting the link below

http://bit.ly/bonus_zalot_cs

***

Conclusion

Thank you again for buying this book!

I hope this book was able to help you understand what astral projection is, and how easy it is to achieve it, even though many people still see it as an unreachable utopia. You should now be able to distinguish between involuntary incidents, such as dreaming, and near death experiences occurring in unconscious states, and astral travel, an out-of-body experience undergone in a conscious state.

Practiced for various reasons throughout history, and widely debated, derided, or aspired to, astral projection is an excellent and unique path to follow in order to deepen your self-awareness, solidify your religious devotion, and shed away all your anxieties. It's the actual proof that our significance extends beyond our mortal lives, and that the feared grand finale is only a permanent spiritual liberation.

By following the specific steps described in this guide, you will surely manage to personally evolve and enhance your psychic, mental, and emotional capacities so as to improve the quality of your life. I wish to accentuate again that astral projection is not an appropriate choice for people with psychological disorders. Other than that, if you have prepared accordingly, no issues should occur, if you take into consideration all its subsequent effects and potential risks.

The next step is to try it for yourself, and live all the enriching benefits arriving from it. All it takes is belief, commitment, and perseverance. As with any meaningful endeavor, astral projection must be carefully planned, studied, and prepared for mentally and physically. Only by means of total dedication, and loyal repetition, our effectiveness can improve and our potential can widen. After all, it is what it takes to attain valuable successes and experiences, of whatever type.

Finally, if you enjoyed this book, then I'd like to ask you for a favor, would you be kind enough to leave a review for this book on Amazon? It'd be greatly appreciated!

Thank you and good luck!

***

Receive e-mail updates on new book releases and free book promotions from Tabitha Zalot. By visiting the link below

http://bit.ly/bonus_zalot_cs

***

Check Out My Other Books

You will find these books by simply searching for them on Amazon.com

Inside this book you will learn how you can use the power of crystals to calm you down when you are feeling stressed out or anxious. You will learn how to harness the healing power of crystals to help you get your calmness and control back again. By using crystals the proper way, you will even be able to get your love life back in balance.

By learning how to unlock your chakras, you will even learn how to prevent diseases. Sound good so far...? Well, why don't you just go ahead and buy your own copy of this book right now? And let's get started with the 7 major chakras and their meanings.

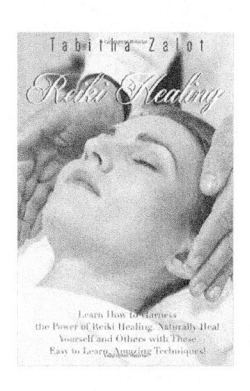

What Reiki healing represents and how it can change your life - The benefits and advantages of Reiki - How to become a Reiki Master - What are the principles, symbols, and techniques of Reiki healing and how they work - How Reiki works on physical, mental, emotional, and spiritual levels - What does a Reiki session involve - And much, much more.

Are You Tired of Feeling Depressed, Stressed, Angry, or Anxious? This book will show you how to get rid of all of your negative feelings in a healthy, natural way. The ancient art of mindfulness can yield immediate results even for people who have never tried it before.

Take a journey all the way to the past, and witness some of the greatest moments in history, read people's auras, and see what happening hundreds of thousands of miles away is. All of that is possible through clairvoyance, and you can find out how to do that by reading this book.

You're about to discover that psychic abilities are not just a taboo myth we heard and feared ever since, but a real fact we should deal with, instead of asking ourselves questions. And because this is not that simple as it seems, this book is going to help you discover and develop your inner psychic abilities and intuition through simple exercises for beginners.

FREE BONUS!

As a special thank you I offer you a free TABITHA ZALOT box set.

This box set contains three life changing e-books and one audiobook.

This is the ultimate box set for anyone committed to know more about the concept of New Age, or anyone interested in Meditation and Mindfulness as a way to create the life, love and happiness you always dreamt about!

Get your copy here: **bit.ly/bonus_zalot_cs**

Greetings from the Lean Stone Publishing Company

We want to thank you so much for reading this book to the end. We are committed to creating life changing books in the Self Help area, such as this one that you just read.

If you liked this book and want to follow us for more information on upcoming book launches, free promotions and special offers, then follow us on Facebook and Twitter!

Sign up for e-mail updates on new releases and free promotions by visiting this link:

http://bit.ly/list_lsp_cs

Like us: **www.facebook.com/leanstonepublishing**

Follow: **@leanstonebooks**

Thank you again for reading to the end, it means the world to us!

Printed in Great Britain
by Amazon